LIVING WITH HORSES
(AND OTHER ANIMALS WHO RUN MY LIFE)

A WITTY MEMOIR
SUE SHELTON-SMITH

About the Author

Sue Shelton-Smith lives in rural Leicestershire with her husband, three horses, and three dogs—though who's really in charge is open to debate. A lifelong rider and devoted animal lover, she has spent decades navigating the joys and absurdities of country life. When not mucking out, she can be found sharing coffee, cake, and laughter with her long-suffering friends and fellow riders. *Living with Horses (and Other Unruly Creatures)* is her first book.

Contents

Introduction: A Willing Hostage   1

1. The Courtship Canter   2
2. Moving to Furneux Pelham   5
3. Children, Ponies, and Other Wild Creatures   7
4. Horses: Why Horses?   10
5. Dogs, Glorious Dogs   19
6. Riding with Friends   25
7. Stable Management
    (Otherwise Known as Hard Labour)   29
8. The Exotic Bit:
    Travel Adventures on Horseback   37
9. The Great Holiday Dilemma   46
10. Growing Older (Gracefully, or Not)   49
11. Pets, Not Servants   51

Epilogue: Under the Same Sky   54

LIVING WITH HORSES (AND OTHER UNRULY CREATURES)

A WITTY MEMOIR BY SUE SHELTON-SMITH

INTRODUCTION: A WILLING HOSTAGE

I never set out to be a zookeeper. And yet here I am, living in a house that smells faintly of hay and dog biscuits, sharing my land with three horses, three dogs, and the ghosts of several dearly departed companions resting under the grass.

People say horse-ownership is a lifestyle. I say it's more like a hostage situation, only with prettier manes. Horses—and dogs—dictate my days, my holidays, and my bank balance. They test my patience, drain my wallet, and break my back. And yet I wouldn't swap it for all the spa weekends in the world.

This is the story of Monty, Izzy, and Dinky (my equine co-stars), the endless parade of dogs, and the human friends who make the chaos survivable. It's also the story of muck heaps, flying hooves, exotic adventures, and why, with age, I now choose coffee and cake or wine, over galloping and hedges.

So, pull on your boots (metaphorically), pour yourself a glass of wine (definitely), and come along for the ride.

Chapter 1: The Courtship Canter

When I first met John, I thought it only fair to introduce him to riding. If he was going to be part of my life, then horses were going to be part of his. At the time, I owned a half-Arab mare called Bay—spirited, clever, and just fiery enough to test a novice.

Since John was bigger than me, I let him ride her, with me astride a comfortable but slow Welsh Cob. He looked surprisingly at ease in the saddle, all confidence and long legs, as though this was going to be his natural element. We set off on a hack near Weston-on-Trent, chatting amiably, the picture of calm domestic bliss.

Then I suggested a canter.

The second Bay's hooves struck the ground, John's confidence evaporated. He was up there in the saddle, but it was Bay who was firmly in charge. She lengthened her stride, lifted her head, and set off as though the Derby bell had just rung. John, meanwhile, flapped along like a flag in the wind, valiantly pretending to be in control.

I shouted instructions—'Sit deep!' 'Steady her up!'—but the gap between us grew with alarming speed. The track climbed a hill and curved sharply at the top. I could just see John's shoulders stiffen as Bay hurtled on. With nothing else to offer, I bellowed, 'Lean into the bend!' as though we were suddenly competing at Brands Hatch.

And then they disappeared from sight.

I pounded up the hill, heart thudding, imagining the carnage of horse and rider parting company in spectacular fashion. But when I rounded the bend, there they were: Bay, standing quietly, reins slack; and John, sitting tall in the saddle, looking insufferably smug. Too smug.

'See? Perfectly fine,' he said, as though he'd planned it all along.

Bay's flicking ears suggested otherwise.

It was my first inkling of John's approach to riding—and, perhaps, to life: lose control entirely, bluff your way through, and then act as if the outcome was exactly what you intended.

Chapter 2: Moving to Furneux Pelham

When we moved to Furneux Pelham in Hertfordshire, I wagered John that he would be the first to end up in hospital. John already had a fine collection of injuries from rugby, climbing and his other adventurous sports, so it seemed only natural that he would soon find his way into a new hospital. It seemed a safe bet.

Life in a horsey village, I explained, is full of hazards for the unsuspecting husband: hooves flying at awkward angles, ponies barging through gateways, Labradors dropping logs in your path. 'It won't be me,' I said confidently. 'It'll be you, so you'd better find out where the nearest one is.'

Naturally, fate took this as a challenge.

One fine morning, I saddled up and headed out, full of optimism. The ride began well enough, until my horse decided to improvise. A little leap here, a sideways shuffle there—and suddenly I was airborne, executing what can only be described as an involuntary dismount.

I landed with a thud, pride dented but otherwise intact still hanging onto the reins—or so I thought. I picked myself up, dusted myself down, and thought I'd got away with nothing worse than bruised pride—until I looked at my hand. My finger was bent at an angle no human joint should attempt. Badly dislocated. Crooked like a banana.

The horse didn't bolt, naturally. He stood there calmly, reins dangling, watching me stagger to my feet with the smug expression only horses can muster. '*Clumsy human,*' his eyes said.

So, it was me—not John—who was bundled off to hospital first. John was insufferably smug about it, of course. 'Didn't you say *I'd* be the one?' he asked sweetly, while I glared at him over my mangled finger.

The moral of the story? Never tempt fate. Especially when horses are involved.

Chapter 3: Children, Ponies, and Other Wild Creatures

People assume that having horse-mad children makes life easier. 'They'll muck out for you,' they said. 'They'll share the work,' they promised. Lies. All lies.

Laura, my eldest, took to riding like she'd been born in the saddle. Her very first pony club fancy dress was a masterpiece: kitted out as a highwayman, complete with tricorn hat and mask, perched proudly on her pony as if Dick Turpin himself had risen from the grave. She was barely tall enough to reach the stirrups, but already she had the air of someone planning her getaway on the Great North Road.

From that day on, ponies became her life. Pony Club rallies, gymkhanas, showjumping competitions—you name it, we were there, usually with the boot of the car stuffed with tack, snacks, and a soggy picnic. I spent years shivering in damp fields, clutching a lukewarm coffee, shouting "Heels down!" while Laura soared over jumps with the concentration of an Olympic athlete. Somewhere along the way, I realised she had become as besotted as I was. The torch had passed, along with the mud but not yet the bills.

Then there was Matthew. If Laura worked hard at it, Matthew simply *'had it'*. He was, without question, the best rider in the household. Horses and dogs adored him, as if recognising a kindred spirit. He could slide onto a pony bareback, no fuss, no fear, and within minutes the animal would be following him like a lamb. Natural talent in spades.

The only problem? He was also the only one of us sensible enough to see that horses came with mucking out, endless chores, and a smell you couldn't wash out of your clothes. And so, after a few too many *'safe hacks'* and mornings with a pitchfork, Matthew quietly bowed out. He discovered skateboards, then girls, and then roller hockey. By the time he was suiting up for the Ashby Aces every weekend with his dad cheering from the sidelines, his jodhpurs were gathering dust in the tack room.

To this day, I maintain he could have been the rider of the family, had he chosen. But perhaps he was wiser than the rest of us. Laura and I were lured into what may have been the lifelong trap of horses. Matthew escaped with wheels on his feet and far fewer vet bills.

Now, of course, the children have grown up and have families of their own.

Laura has long since left horses behind but gained something far better—her wonderful daughter, **Evie**, who already shows the sparkle and spirit that once made her mother such a determined little rider.

And as for Matthew, he vowed that neither he nor his family would ever get caught up in *'the horse set.'* Yet I can't help but watch with curiosity to see how daughter **Cali** fares—and with a newborn named **Kayce**, well, surely that's a cowboy in the making?

After all, I live in hope. Perhaps one day, I'll find myself back at a gymkhana, cheering on a new generation, proudly parading the little ones on a small pony, just as we once did all those years ago.

CHAPTER 4: HORSES. WHY HORSES?

It's a question I ask myself regularly, usually when I'm knee-deep in mud or staring at a vet bill that looks suspiciously like a mortgage payment.

Why horses?

They smell. They kick. They poo with industrial efficiency. They weigh half a ton and somehow still manage to injure themselves in empty fields with nothing to trip over. And yet, despite all of this, like some sort of equine Stockholm Syndrome—I can't quit them, and I'm now shackled to three of them.

Monty comes first. He's the sort of horse who lulls you into a false sense of security. Big, brown, soft-eyed, gentle as a lamb. A horse you'd describe as 'safe.' Which is precisely why Monty is, on the surface, a gentleman. His eyes are soft, his nose like velvet, his walk slow and steady. Strangers pat him and murmur, *'Oh, isn't he kind?'* and I nod politely, because it seems unkind to say, *'Well, yes, until he tries to kill my husband.'*

It was Christmas day, and all the family were round for a special meal, cooking was virtually complete and wine was breathing. 'You go and fetch the horses in and I'll get changed.' I said. John all dressed in his Christmas shirt and bright trousers wandered out to the field with lead reins. Izzy was the first in and well behaved. Next Monty who was sharing a pasture with Dinky. Dinky the rascal shot around the electric fence and just as John was fastening the lead rein,

Monty decided to follow, twisting John around before kicking him with the force of a piston in his back.

There was a loud *thwack*, a startled yelp, and suddenly my husband was on the floor gasping like a landed fish. This was all unbeknown to us all waiting to go off to the pub for a Christmas drink until finally John wheezed his way into the lounge.

'Are you all right?' I asked, in the sort of tone that suggested I might laugh at any second.
'No,' he wheezed, clutching his back. 'Your horse just tried to kill me.'
Monty out in the field neighing, blinking innocently, and snorting as if to say, '*Don't drag me into this.*' What followed was a rush to hospital, a major operation and a stay in Intensive Care for John between Christmas and New Year! He now carries the scars of battle and two Titanium ribs and relishes telling anyone about the incident who wants to hear.

To this day, John refuses to walk behind Monty. Fair enough, I suppose. That incident cemented Monty's reputation in the family. Not as a villain, but as the sort of horse who lulls you into a false sense of security, then reminds you—politely but firmly—that a half-ton of muscle will always win.

Monty has other tricks, of course. He has perfected the art of 'strategic immobility.' You lead him out to the field, and halfway there he stops. No amount of cajoling, pleading, or bribery will shift him. He plants his hooves like he's auditioning for a statue competition, and there he remains, until he decides otherwise. Once, I left him standing there while I went to fetch a lead rope. When I came back, he was still in the same spot, dozing peacefully. I sometimes wonder if Monty secretly works as a mindfulness coach, teaching humans the virtue of stillness.

His appetite is another menace. Monty can detect a carrot in a pocket from thirty yards away. He once unzipped John's coat with his lips and helped himself to a packet of mints. He has also, on more than one occasion, eaten the shrubs outside of his stable and even tried eating the hosepipe.

And yet—despite the bruises, the stubbornness, the larceny—Monty is, somehow, adored. He is the steady one in traffic, the calm presence when Izzy spins like a ballerina on amphetamines, the horse that children gravitate towards. He may be a menace, but he's *our* menace.

John still eyes him suspiciously, of course. Whenever Monty flicks a tail, John instinctively sidesteps like a matador. I tell him it's character building. John tells me it's grounds for divorce.

But here's the truth: Monty is not really malicious. He's simply a large, occasionally clumsy, often hungry horse, with a very dry sense of humour. And, if you ask me, that makes him the most human member of the family.

Monty, the kind horse, delivered a near-fatal blow to John.

Izzy the Diva is the horse equivalent of a faded actress who refuses to believe she's past her prime. Once upon a time, she was bred to be a racehorse. Unfortunately, Izzy couldn't run to save her life. On the track, she was less 'thoroughbred race machine' and more 'confused deer caught in headlights.' When the starting gates opened, she apparently thought, *After*

you, darling. Needless to say, she was retired from racing early.

We tried dressage instead. Some days she floats across the arena, neck arched, hooves tapping rhythmically, prancing like a ballerina, and flicking her tail as though she's performing at the Royal Opera House. I've seen her float across an arena with such grace that strangers applauded.

Other days, she spooks at her own shadow and does an impromptu impression of a drunken camel. I once tried to impress a dressage judge by showing off her 'extended trot.' Izzy extended, all right—straight out of the arena and into the car park.

But then there are the other days. Days when she takes one look at a dressage marker, decides it is the portal to another dimension, and leaps sideways in horror. Days when a plastic bag flapping in the hedge convinces her that death is imminent. On these occasions, her 'dressage' looks less like artistry and more like interpretive dance, performed by a very angry giraffe.

Her signature move is the 'Oh-no-you-didn't pirouette,' executed when she disagrees with my riding instructions. She spins, I cling on, the audience gasps, and Izzy struts off looking smug.

Izzy also has a knack for holding grudges. Once, I dared to shorten her schooling session. She spent the next week refusing to walk in straight lines, swerving left every few steps in protest. Another time, John tried to lead her out to the field. She dragged him through a hedge and left him stuck there, like a badly dressed scarecrow.

IZZY, THE FAILED RACEHORSE

And yet, for all her theatrics, Izzy is loved. She keeps Monty from getting too lazy, challenges me to stay alert, and entertains friends with her endless dramatics. Deep down, I suspect Izzy doesn't really want to be a dressage horse. She wants to be a leading lady. Sadly, the West End hasn't yet created a role for 'Horse Who Refuses to Cooperate.'

And then there's Dinky.

Dinky is a pony. A *small* pony. Bought in as a sensible companion for Monty and Izzy, so they wouldn't be lonely. Instead, Dinky staged a coup. Within weeks he was boss of the yard, marching around with his tiny legs, ears pinned, eyes glinting like a gangster.

He may be little, but he has the self-confidence of Napoleon. Monty—sixteen hands of muscle—backs out of his way. Izzy—supposedly a thoroughbred athlete—lets him steal her food. Dinky takes what he wants, when he wants it, and if challenged, he squeals and lashes out like a toddler in a toy shop.

I've learned to respect him. In fact, we all have.

So, why horses? Because life with them is never dull. They test your patience, drain your bank account, and leave you exhausted. But they also make you laugh, keep you humble, and every so often, remind you what joy looks like. Even if that joy comes in the form of a tiny tyrant named Dinky.

Chapter 5: Dogs, Glorious Dogs

If you thought the horses ran the show, let me introduce you to the dogs.

The current line-up:

Briony (or Brian as John calls her) is our stately old Labrador. Her joints stiff, her eyes cloudy—but food is her focus on life. She moves slowly, with a regal dignity, and if anyone dares to hurry her, she fixes them with a sorrowful look that says, *'What do you want now.'*

Her favourite pastimes are sleeping and eating. Despite her age, she has maintained a selective deafness. 'Dinner?' She hears instantly. 'Walk?' Her ears prick up before the word has even formed. But 'Come here' or 'Be quick' (A term used for enforced toiletry acts) - Nothing. Silence. Apparently, the royal family doesn't take commands.

Visitors adore her. She sits quietly by their feet, head tilted, sighing dramatically like a character in *Downton Abbey*. People tell me she's 'so well behaved.' They don't see her later, sneaking into the kitchen to help herself to whatever's left unattended on the counter. Once, she ate half a birthday cake. Another time, she dragged an entire roast chicken into her bed. Regal, yes. Honest, no.

But Briony is a queen who has earned her crown. She has been there through all the chaos, all the barking, all the galloping, quietly holding the household together with her calm Labrador loyalty. A monarch in fur.

If Briony is royalty, then **Charlie**—our French Bulldog—is the court jester. She snores like a chainsaw, grunts like a pig, and insists on always sitting in laps, regardless of whether those laps belong to guests who came dressed in black trousers.

Charlie doesn't walk; she struts. She waddles like a tiny bodybuilder, chest puffed out, head high, as if to say, '*Yes, I am magnificent. Admire me.*' Unfortunately, her magnificence is often undermined by her tendency to trip over her own paws.

She has a special talent for comedic timing. During serious conversations, Charlie farts loudly and unapologetically. When I'm trying to concentrate, she taps me on the back of my leg or bounces up with a slobbery toy, drops it in my lap, and stares until I comply. And at night, when peace finally reigns, Charlie begins her snoring symphony, a performance so loud it rattles the windows. She insists on sleeping in positions that defy both logic and gravity. She sleeps in improbable positions—on her back, legs in the air, tongue dangling out like she's auditioning for a cartoon.

John claims he can't stand the noise. Yet I often catch him scratching Charlie's ears, muttering, '*Who's a good girl then?*' The answer, of course, is 'Not Charlie.' But we pretend anyway.

Charlie is not useful. She doesn't herd, she doesn't guard, and he certainly doesn't obey. But she makes us laugh every single day. And sometimes, laughter is the most useful thing of all.

Dobby, our rescue Podenco from Spain, has the haunted eyes of a dog who remembers hardship. He is wiry, fast, and clever. Very clever. Too clever, in fact. Dobby has turned stealing into an art form.

Nothing is safe. Socks vanish. Shoes disappear. Tea towels go missing. But Dobby's pièce de résistance is food theft and the art of counter surfing. He once leapt onto the counter and ran off with a whole bunch of bananas which we thought were well out of reach. We returned home to find a smug looking dog, surrounded by banana skins all over the floor, all bananas neatly peeled. Another time, he unzipped my handbag and extracted a bag of cough sweets with the delicacy of a safecracker. Roast chicken left on the kitchen worktop is just a sign saying *steal me*. He's even sprung the art of turning on the TV when left alone just to cheer up the dog household ensuring the volume is so high it can be heard out in the yard. The latest comedic act is to turn on the kitchen tap when everyone is out. This then floods the kitchen floor requiring a mop and bucket. Perhaps a timely message to get me to clean the floor more frequently.

Despite his criminal record, Dobby is deeply affectionate. He creeps onto the sofa and curls up small, pressing himself against you as though trying to make up for every cold night he ever endured. His loyalty is fierce, his love absolute—just don't leave your sandwich unattended.

People often ask if he's 'settled in now.' I laugh. Settled, yes. Reformed? Absolutely not. Dobby is part dog, part thief, part shadow. And I wouldn't change him for the world.

The ghosts of past dogs linger too. There was Jake, the Jack Russell, perhaps the most loved of them all. A tiny dog with the courage of a lion who thought he was ten feet tall and had the stubbornness of ten mules.

Agora and Flacca, two more Spanish Podencos, sweet and skittish in equal measure.

Millie, my faithful black Labrador, who never quite grew out of puppyhood.

And Eric, our very first lovable mongrel—the dog who started it all, who set the standard for chaos.

They're all buried in the garden now, resting beneath the grass, but I still feel their presence. Sometimes, when I'm out in the flower beds, I catch myself expecting Jake to come bounding up, ball in mouth, ready for another throw. Some might find it morbid. I find it comforting. When I walk past, I say hello. Sometimes, I swear I hear tails wagging.

The dogs, like the horses, are less 'pets' and more 'family.' They fill the house with noise, fur, muddy pawprints, and joy. And they remind me—daily—that life is better when you share it with creatures who love you unconditionally… even if they also chew your slippers.

CHAPTER 6: RIDING WITH FRIENDS

Riding, if we're honest, is rarely about the horses. It's about the people you ride with. The gossip, the laughter, the snacks. The horses are simply transport—very large, very expensive bicycles with attitudes.

Take Julia. A lovely rider, graceful and calm, until she had her unfortunate 'unscheduled dismount.' She wasn't badly hurt—just winded, embarrassed, and covered in mud. But the fall marked the end of Julia's riding career. She announced, with a dramatic flair, that she was 'done with horses.' and would be devoting herself to safer pursuits. Like Pilates or making curtains.

We still see each other, of course. She comes round for coffee, brings cake, and tells me how much better life is without muck, manure, or the constant risk of being catapulted into a hedge. I nod politely while brushing hay off my jumper, knowing she'll never come back to the saddle. Julia didn't just fall off her horse that day—she fell into a life of clean clothes and sanity. Lucky woman.

Debbie is another story. Once a dependable hack partner, she suddenly reappeared one spring with what she called 'a new look.' Gone were the muddy jodhpurs and sensible boots. In their place: immaculate hair, gleaming nails, and makeup that could survive a hurricane and a youthful face that may be the result of some work with a scalpel. Sometimes I suspect she's headed to a nightclub rather than a hack through the fields. 'Going riding?' I asked, eyeing her sparkly top.
'Of course,' she said, flipping her hair.
We trotted down the lane and within ten minutes she looked

like she'd been dragged backwards through a compost heap. To her credit, she still insisted she'd never felt more glamorous!

Julie, on the other hand, barely pretends to ride anymore. She shows up in riding gear, yes—but the horse is simply a means of getting out of the house. She is technically a rider, though in practice she's more of a coffee-drinker who occasionally climbs onto a horse. Our *'rides'* often end with a coffee, where we dismount not because the horses are tired, but because we want cake. She insists this is a vital part of the equestrian lifestyle. I can't entirely disagree. 'It's not gossip,' she insists. 'It's *therapy.'* I nod. Therapy that happens to involve cake.

Amy is different. She's young enough to be my daughter—in fact she's more like my surrogate daughter, truth be told. Full of enthusiasm and energy, which is refreshing when the rest of us are creaking our way past middle age. Amy is the youngest of my riding circle, and by far the bravest. Where the rest of us see a hedge and think, *'No thank you, I like my spine,'* Amy sees a hedge and thinks, *'Challenge accepted.'* She is also blessed with the ability to bounce. Amy falls off more often than anyone I know, and yet she springs back up, laughing, brushing herself off, and remounting before I've even unclipped my helmet. Riding with Amy makes me feel younger—until the next day, when my back disagrees. She keeps me on my toes, reminding me what it felt like to be fearless and bendy enough to dismount without grunting.

And then there's Stuart. Stuart is not just a rider; he's an entertainer. Our fabulously funny gay chap. He doesn't ride with me that often now, but when he does, he has more stories than the BBC archives and delivers them with such flamboyance that even the horses seem to listen. He fills the air with stories that make me cry with laughter. Some are scandalous, some are outrageous, and some involve details I couldn't possibly write down. He claims he only comes for the horses, but I strongly suspect it's the wine afterwards.

Stuart is my tonic. When rides are muddy, when horses are stubborn, when morale is low, Stuart swoops in with a story so outrageous that I forget the rain, the mud, and even the aching thighs. Every riding group needs a Stuart. I'm just lucky I've got the original.

Victoria Thurlby, or VJ as she is known, is another surrogate daughter who has expertise and a yearn for great things. She now lives away in Suffolk with her partner Wheelie but does pop in from time to time. In the days when she lived local, she turned up to help train the racehorse Izzy in things all to do with dressage. I just used to sit on a barrel by the menage chatting away while VJ operated the normally wayward horse perfectly. 'You do know horses have a slot in their necks that need you to pop £20 notes in to make them perform, don't you?' she used to say. And yes, into the handbag for another crisp note before she dismounts and readies herself for another coffee.

Together, we form a peculiar kind of horse rambling club. We appear less of a riding partnership and more of a travelling coffee morning with occasional trots. Our 'hacks' are 40% riding, 60% laughter, and 100% chaos. We set out across the countryside, chatting, laughing, occasionally remembering to steer the horses. It's less '*hunt the fox across the fields*' and more '*moving picnic with hooves.*'

And honestly, I wouldn't have it any other way.

Chapter 7: Stable Management (Otherwise Known as Hard Labour)

Let me tell you: running a yard looks very romantic in glossy horse magazines. Gleaming horses, tidy stables, happy owners beaming in spotless breeches. The reality? Think less *Downton Abbey*, more *Prison Break with manure*. In reality, I spend 90% of my horse life staring at the business end of a wheelbarrow.

The stables face into our courtyard, which means Monty, Izzy, and Dinky spend a lot of time watching me with what I can only describe as judgemental stares. They know the routine better than I do: breakfast at dawn (or earlier, if they can bang on the doors loud enough), fields during the day, back inside by evening, dinner precisely on time or else.

It's less about horsemanship and more about being a short-order chef for animals with very strict dietary requirements.

Mucking out? Horses poo with the efficiency of factories. Monty's stable alone could supply a small power station. Izzy waits for the farrier's visit to deposit hers, while Dinky takes pride in pooing in his water bucket.

Grooming should be soothing. Instead, Monty leans so hard I nearly topple over, Izzy tolerates me with disdain, and Dinky tries to bite the brush.

Fence management? Monty once undid the gate somehow (I couldn't have left it open!) and led a raid into the neighbour's garden. Munching on the trees and well-groomed bushes, all the while looking smug. I did manage to retrieve them before Ken noticed the damage was caused by my horses, and when I did see him, 'Ken, that's a mess. Alice's horses escaped again?' I said turning away sheepishly.

Horses eat more than teenage boys. And hay bales are deceptively heavy—farmers stack them with glee, knowing full well we'll spend the winter hauling them around like unpaid strongmen.

Let's not forget the décor. Each year the stables must be repainted. This isn't decorating. It's surrender. Horses redecorate daily with mud, teeth marks, and mysterious stains. An annual event that marks the turning of the seasons as Spring emerges from the depths of Winter.

And then there's Simon, the farrier—Julie's husband, and practically family by now. Every six weeks, he trims, shoes, and politely ignores my panic about having the right cash. Dinky, naturally, tries to bite him but Simon still comes back. That's friendship.

Exhausting, filthy, relentless—but when the yard is clean and the horses munch happily, it feels oddly glorious.

MUCKING OUT: THE GYM MEMBERSHIP NOBODY ASKED FOR

Take mucking out. This sounds quaint until you realise it means shovelling mountains of manure with the enthusiasm of a condemned miner. By barrow number four, I've usually questioned all my life choices. By number six, I'm hallucinating about clean floors. Non-horse people imagine it's just sweeping up. No. It's industrial-scale shovelling. Some people pay for gym memberships. I shovel manure. Every morning, without fail, armed with a fork and a wheelbarrow that has a wheel designed to wobble dangerously, I begin the noble art of mucking out.

It is not glamorous. The magazines show shiny stables with golden straw. Mine look like a scene from *Les Misérables*, only smellier. Monty produces droppings the size of cannonballs. Izzy scatters hers like confetti. Dinky, bless him, manages to poo in every corner simultaneously, defying the laws of physics. On top of this, they all delight in squirting vast quantities of foul-smelling pee onto freshly laid straw.

The wheelbarrow, of course, is always overloaded. I tell myself this is strength training. My back disagrees. Once, I tipped the barrow too early and ended up wearing half the load down my trousers. John offered to buy me a Fitbit once. I told him my muck heap is my Fitbit.

It is endless, thankless, back-breaking work. And yet—oddly satisfying. There is something cleansing about starting the day with a fresh stable, a happy horse, and the faint hope that tomorrow they might poo less. (Spoiler: they never do.)

POO-PICKING: ZEN AND THE ART OF SHOVELLING

This is essentially '*Wheelbarrow CrossFit*.' If mucking out is hard labour, poo-picking is meditation. Out in the field, armed with a scoop and wheelbarrow, I wander like a pilgrim, searching for droppings. The horses watch me,

chewing grass, clearly amused. Field poo-picking is a special kind of torture. I once had a neighbour lean over the gate and call, 'You know, they sell that stuff in bags at the garden centre!' Ha. Ha. Very funny. Nothing boosts one's dignity like waving at passing neighbours while wielding a pitchfork.

Dinky likes to follow me, occasionally knocking over the barrow so I have to start again. Monty shadows me like a supervisor, as though checking the quality of my work. Izzy pretends not to know me, too embarrassed by my efforts.

Friends say it must be mind-numbing. In truth, there's something peaceful about it. It's quiet, it's steady, and it's oddly satisfying to see a clean patch of field behind you. Sometimes I even hum or sing the latest song our lady's choir is tackling, that is until the barrow tips over and the cycle begins again.

Fence Management: Houdini in Reverse

Fence management is another delight. Horses don't escape because they're desperate—they escape because they *can*. Monty once discovered he could lean on a fence post until it snapped. He led Izzy and Dinky into next door's fields, where they ate the lush green grass. When confronted, Monty had the gall to look surprised, Izzy looked smug, and Dinky simply belched.

The Farrier: Six-Weekly Financial Ruin

And then, of course, there's Simon, the farrier. He turns up every six weeks with his tools, calm patience, and a knack for avoiding Dinky's teeth. He's Julie's husband, which means I can't scare him off—I need him too much. He's practically family now, which is good, because I've paid him so often, he may as well declare me a dependent on his tax return -- if he does one.

Simon is an ex-rodeo rider and thinks he is a reincarnated cowboy. I can't help but think he's correct.

Every visit follows the same routine: Tea, normal with just one sugar, then as he trims and shoes while Monty tries to bite his backside. I attempt polite conversation but then, 'Where's John?' he asks hoping for some male conversation. So, I take the hint and go off to search through my pockets for the right amount of cash. And still, somehow, Simon comes back.

Monty and Izzy get new shoes. Dinky gets a hoof trim. I get a lighter wallet. It's a ritual. Simon bends, hammers, and clips, the horses sigh, and I stand by trying not to faint at the bill. 'It's the price of sound horses,' Simon says cheerfully, as though that helps.

The horses adore him. They generally stand still, ears pricked, behaving better for Simon than they ever do for me. It's infuriating. I once suggested he should move in and handle them full-time. Julie vetoed the idea.

Still, Simon has become a friend. We see him more than most relatives. We gossip while he works, he offers unsolicited advice about fencing, and occasionally we even talk about horses. Then he hands me the bill, and I briefly consider selling Dinky to the circus. As an aside, he has tried to organise an annual Shackerstone Conker Contest and soon a Worm Charming championship. Clearly a man of many talents.

IN SUMMARY:

It's relentless, filthy, exhausting. But here's the thing: when I step back, look at the freshly swept yard, the horses munching happily, the smell of hay in the air—I love it. In a masochistic way.

Chapter 8: The Exotic Bit (Travel Adventures on Horseback)

Despite being chained to the yard, I've managed to escape on riding holidays. (Thank you, Sam Pallet, patron saint of house-sitters.) On paper, these trips sound glamorous: galloping with gauchos, rounding up cattle, riding through the Okavango Delta. In reality? Less *equestrian goddess*, more, *slightly terrified middle-aged woman clinging on for dear life*.

California Ranch: Not quite Butch Cassidy and the Sundance Kid but Close.

Initially when the kids were young enough to go away with us and still capable of riding (Matthew being perhaps the most natural horse rider of us all) we ventured across to the Rockies and Hunewill Ranch in California.

Riding out like cowboys twice a day galloping through the small lakes and pretending we were cavalry charging across the plains. But it was here that we had our first experience of a medical disaster.

Matthew playing in a stream got hit on the head by a rock thrown by some other child. Blood everywhere and the nearest medical facility was at least 100 miles away. No worry, it's a ranch. With a family of doctors and nurses holidaying, supplies of ketamine (horse anaesthetic) and some good strong thread, the team set to stitching him up by the light of a bedside lamp held aloft. A celebrity and star for the rest of the holiday with horse bandage around his head making him look like a real hero and excusing him from having to wear a cowboy hat. Aware of his celebrity status, he now revelled in skateboarding off the veranda of the cabin we were staying in with his jeans hanging precariously off his backside and his underpants bare for all to see!

But there's one big gripe I have from this trip: Each week the ranch holds a day of competitive riding and John, despite having little riding experience came out as the champion rider for that week. I say he beat me by cheating and causing me to have an injury. I've tried to hide his trophy, but he keeps pulling it out when horsey guests arrive! I won't say any more about the event as it obviously hurts.

ARGENTINA: THE GALLOP THAT NEVER ENDED

Argentina promised wide-open spaces, fast horses, and gauchos, who looked like they'd stepped straight out of a film set. It delivered all three, plus more beef than any human could reasonably consume in one lifetime.

The riding was extraordinary. The gauchos rode effortlessly, legs hanging loose, reins barely touched and set off at a flat-out gallop across terrain that looked suspiciously like a broken ankle waiting to happen. 'Vamos!' they shouted. I went, all right—though my scream echoed across the pampas. By the time we stopped, my thighs felt like they'd been attacked with a blowtorch. The gaucho grinned and handed me a flask of something that stripped the enamel off my teeth.

Stopping was not optional. In fact, it wasn't even possible. My horse galloped until it decided otherwise, ignoring my increasingly desperate attempts at brakes. I briefly considered shouting 'Taxi!' and rolling off, but pride stopped me. Eventually, the horse halted at a small stream, lowering his head to drink as though nothing unusual had happened looking at me as if to say, *Problem?*

Evenings were filled with asados—giant barbecues where entire cows appeared to be roasted at once. Plates groaned under piles of meat, washed down with Malbec. By day three, I was convinced my arteries had solidified, but I didn't care. Argentina was glorious, terrifying, delicious and utterly unforgettable. I came home with thighs that didn't belong, and arteries probably lined with steak fat—but also with the bragging rights of surviving the pampas at full gallop.

Wyoming: Playing at Cowboys

In Wyoming, I fancied myself a cowgirl. I bought the hat, the boots, even attempted a swagger. The horse, however, was unimpressed.

Western horses are supposed to be calm, steady, and sensible. Mine had other ideas. When faced with actual cattle, he decided he wanted no part of the enterprise. While the others herded cows like professionals, my horse spun in circles, snorting in protest, as if to say, *'Nope. I'm unionised. Cows aren't in my contract.'* At lunch, one of them asked politely if I'd considered, 'maybe a smaller horse?' I pretended not to hear.

Wyoming was different from California, cowboys, real ones, with weather-beaten faces and the casual confidence of men who've been in the saddle since birth. They handed me a lariat, expecting me to learn roping in ten minutes. I gave it a whirl—literally—and managed to lasso my own boot. 'You ain't from around here, are you?' one cowboy drawled. Astute observation.

Still, Wyoming was magnificent. The mountains, the clear skies, the sense of space—it was like stepping into a film. I never quite achieved the cowgirl fantasy, but I did manage to sit a Western saddle for five hours without crying. Which, in my book, counts as success.

BOTSWANA: LIONS, ELEPHANTS, AND A HORSE WITH NO BRAKES

But Africa—ah, Africa. Magical, terrifying, unforgettable. We rode through the Okavango, water up to the horses' bellies, birds flapping overhead, giraffes watching from the trees. Once, we startled a herd of elephants, who trumpeted their annoyance. Our horses froze. My heart nearly stopped. Then someone whispered, 'Is that a hippo?' At which point, the mood shifted from *'Out of Africa'* to *'Every woman for herself.'*

We had a man with a rifle riding behind us, 'Just in case.' Just in case of *what* was never specified. Lion? Leopard? Crocodile? I didn't ask. I simply smiled politely and pretended to be brave, while quietly rehearsing my obituary in my head. I didn't sleep well that night.

Botswana was breathtaking. Galloping through shallow water, flocks of birds exploding into the sky, zebra and

giraffe galloping alongside—it felt like stepping into a David Attenborough documentary, only sweatier.

Of course, my horse had his own agenda. In the middle of a heroic gallop, he would slam on the brakes to eat grass. So, while everyone else charged into the distance, I was left behind shouting, '*Not now!*' as he munched happily. The safari guide nearly fell off laughing.

Then there was Belinda who we'd met on a trip before. She was a wiry old cuss from Wyoming and in the winter was reported to have been an Ice Road Trucker. Not an ounce of meat on her but tough as old boots. One day she thought it a great idea to charge off with Zebra while filming from her camera. That was until the horse needed to jump over an old tree. Then it was a change of transport as she sailed through

the air like a bald eagle looking for prey. Landing wasn't a smooth descent and certainly less graceful resulting in an audible *snap* as bones submitted to the hard earth. Hospital was a long way off and special arrangements made, but this didn't deter her as she continued the dangerous exploits once back out of plaster and slings. Mad Woman!

But the best parts? Evenings around the fire with Kim, Julie, and the gang. Wine, laughter, exaggerations, and aching muscles. Those memories fuel me through endless wheelbarrows of manure.

Nights were no calmer. Heading to our tents listening to lions roar in the distance. The horses dozed nearby, unfazed. I, on the other hand, brushed my teeth to the sound of a hippo grunting outside the tent and mentally drafted my obituary: '*Leicestershire Woman Attacked While Quietly Cleaning Her Teeth.*'

Botswana remains my favourite. Wild, exhilarating, and the perfect reminder that however ridiculous my horses at home may be, at least they don't share a field with lions.

The reality of these trips? Less *'equestrian goddess,'* more *'slightly terrified middle-aged woman clinging on for dear life.'*

Do I come home with sunburn, bruises, and a questionable limp? Yes. Do I also come home with memories that make the daily mucking out bearable? Absolutely.

Still, I'd do it all again. These trips weren't really about the riding—they were about the friends who came with me. Kim, Julie, and the gang from *In the Saddle*. We laughed ourselves silly in the evenings, wine flowing freely as we compared bruises and exaggerated our bravery.

Traveling on horseback in far-off lands makes our village hacks look tame. But honestly, give me a sunny afternoon, a good gossip, and a slice of cake at the café, and I'm just as happy.

CHAPTER 9: THE GREAT HOLIDAY DILEMMA

Holidays. Such a simple concept for normal people. They book a flight, pack a suitcase, maybe throw a few plants at the neighbour and call it done.

For me? Holidays are a logistical nightmare that require military precision.

First, the dogs. They can't be kennelled. (Briony would pine, Charlie would probably be evicted for snoring, and Dobby would escape through a ventilation shaft within 24 hours.) Then the horses. Monty, Izzy, and Dinky have zero survival instincts—they need feeding, turning out, mucking out, rugs changed, water buckets filled, and the occasional cuddle.

Holidays, for normal people, mean sun, cocktails, and relaxation. For me, they mean panic, lists, and the desperate hunt for someone brave enough to care for the animals. Which is why I thank the universe for Sam Pallet: saint, heroine, and the only person on earth I trust not to let Dinky stage a coup while I'm away.

Sam takes it all in stride, bless her. She manages the chaos, the barking, the manure, and even sends reassuring texts. I still spend half my holiday worrying, of course, but thanks to Sam, I can at least gallop past elephants in Botswana knowing the real zoo at home is under control.

Sam is our house sitter, our guardian angel. She knows her way around a wheelbarrow, isn't fazed by dog hair, and can deal with Dinky's attitude without bursting into tears. I've left her notes before, but honestly, Sam could write them

better than I could. 'Feed horses, feed dogs, try not to get killed'—that's the gist. Before each trip, I write Sam an instruction manual. It grows every year. Feeding times, quirks, warning signs, emergency contacts. By now, it resembles the Dead Sea Scrolls. 'Don't let Dobby near to food, keep all parcels out of reach and secure the kitchen before you leave each day. Monty sulks if fed last. Izzy mustn't be tied next to Dinky unless you enjoy carnage.'

And while I'm away, lounging under the African sun or pretending to be a cowgirl in Wyoming, part of me is always thinking: *Did Monty finish his hay? Did Charlie find the warmest patch of sofa? Did Dinky stage another coup?*

Most people worry about leaving the oven on. I worry about whether the farrier will show up while I'm in another hemisphere.

But when you're finally away—truly away—it's bliss. No poo-picking. No hay lifting. No chasing dogs through the neighbour's vegetable patch. Just sun on your face, wine in your hand, and the smug glow of knowing that back home, Sam has everything under control. That's my idea of paradise.

Chapter 10: Growing Older (Gracefully, or Not)

There comes a time in every rider's life when the thought sneaks in: *'What if I fall?'* You look at a hedge and instead of thinking, *'I can jump that'*, you think, *'Why on earth would I want to?'*

In your twenties, you bounce. In fact, it's almost a badge of honour. In your thirties, it was inconvenient and you bruise. In your forties, you limp and it's getting very painful. Now, in my... well, let's say *later years*, you know a fall could mean three months explaining yourself to the NHS.

I wasn't always cautious. In younger days, I thought nothing of charging over hedges, splashing through rivers, flying at ditches with reckless abandon. Now? Now I eye a small log on the ground and think, *Hmm. Best go around that.*

These days, my rides are sedate rambles. Country lanes, gentle canters, lots of talking, very little risk. Sometimes we don't even trot if the ground looks 'a bit uneven.' Monty approves—his joints creak like an old wardrobe. Izzy's joints stiffen on cold mornings and she's happy to dawdle. We're all slowing down together, creaking along in unison.

Our rides have slowed to a gentle plod. And you know what? I don't mind. There's a quiet pleasure in ambling down country lanes, chatting with friends, letting the horses stretch their legs without breaking a sweat. No trophies, no speed, no risks—just the companionship of horse, rider, and the occasional nosy sheep.

There's also the indignity of dismounting. In my youth, I swung gracefully off the saddle. Now, I slide down like a sack of flour and hope my knees catch me before the ground does. Monty once gave me a withering look that clearly said, *'Honestly, woman.'*

But do I miss the thrill? Sometimes. Then I remember my friend Kim, who once attempted a heroic hedge-jump, missed, and ended up in the ditch shouting, 'Don't let anyone take photos!' I laughed so hard I nearly joined her.

No, I'm happy with slow and steady. Besides, there's no glory in being airlifted from a bridleway. Not when there's a café at the end of the lane serving scones.

Chapter 11: Pets, Not Servants

Once upon a time, horses were tools. They ploughed fields, pulled carts, carried soldiers into battle. Dogs, too, were workers—ratters, hunters, guards.

Not here. Not anymore.

Monty, Izzy, and Dinky are not '*servants.*' They're spoiled, pampered pets who happen to eat like elephants. Their days of work are behind them (or in Dinky's case, never really existed). They've become companions, friends, part of the family.

Monty spends his days being adored. Izzy demands massages, special feeds, and rugs changed more often than a toddler's pyjamas. Dinky, meanwhile, eats his bodyweight in hay and bullies everyone—including me. None of them '*work.*' They're companions, comedians, occasionally therapists.

The dogs too. They no longer '*earn their keep.*' Unless you count Charlie's talent for keeping the sofa warm, or Briony's ability to lick a plate clean providing quiet wisdom—and the occasional puddle when her bladder forgets itself. Dobby has an impressive guard-dog routine when a leaf blows past the window and keeps us sharp on not leaving food out.

As time passes, of course, each beloved creature eventually makes their way to the garden. Beneath the grass, in the quiet corner of the lawn or the field, they rest. Horses, dogs, all of them together. It sounds sad, but it isn't—not really. It's comforting. A reminder that they're still here, still part of the land, still part of us. As they grow old, their roles change. They're less about what they can *do* and more about who they *are*. Each has a personality, a soul, a place in our family.

And when their time comes, they join the others in the garden. Beneath the grass, under the old tree, lie Jake, my scrappy Jack Russell with the heart of a lion. Agora and Flacca, the soulful Podencos. Millie, the gentle black Lab. Eric, our very first mongrel, who taught me more about loyalty than any human ever could. Horses too, when their day arrives head out into the field for the last time. It sounds sad, but it isn't. I like knowing they're close, still part of the land, still part of us.

Each one rests beneath the grass, but none are truly gone. On quiet evenings, when the horses are tucked up and the air smells of hay, I can almost feel them at my side again. A rustle in the leaves, a phantom paw at my heel, a memory so strong it becomes presence.

It's not sadness I feel, but gratitude. To have shared my life with so many animals is a privilege few are lucky enough to know.

And so, every morning, I drag myself out of bed, pull on the wellies, and head to the yard. Muck out, feed, groom, repair, repeat. And every evening, I collapse into a chair surrounded by dogs, with hay in my hair and mud on my trousers.

It's hard, it's chaotic, it's relentless. But for all the chaos, for all the bruises, for all the expense and the endless wheelbarrows of poo… this life is mine.

But it's also joy.

And truthfully? I wouldn't trade it for all the tidy holidays, clean houses, or peaceful lie-ins in the world.

Epilogue: Under the Same Sky

When I was young, horses were for riding. Dogs were for guarding or fetching. Animals had jobs, and we had expectations. Now, those boundaries have dissolved. Monty and Izzy are less my 'mounts' and more my companions. The dogs, whether old or young, are less guardians and more family.

They are no longer here to serve me. I am here to serve them. To feed, to care, to soothe, to sit quietly in their company. And in return, they give me something far more valuable than work: they give me their presence, their trust, and their love.

It is a strange, beautiful shift—to grow older alongside your animals, to see them not as tools but as equals in the long, messy, hilarious story of a shared life.

People sometimes ask when I'll 'Give it all up?' The truth? I won't. Not willingly.

Because every hoofbeat, every muddy pawprint, every farrier bill and hay bale has stitched itself into the fabric of my life.

I may be a hostage to horses and dogs, but I'm a willing one.

And, honestly, I wouldn't want parole.

One day, Monty, Izzy, and even little Dinky will join the others under the grass. I know this. But for now, we carry on together, creaky joints and all, plodding down lanes, gossiping with friends, and laughing at Stuart's endless stories.

There's a comfort in the rhythm of it all: the mucking out, the farrier visits, the rides, the dogs underfoot, the horses waiting at the gate. It is work, yes, but it is also joy. And if joy comes with mud on your boots and hay in your hair, then I'll gladly wear both.

Because at the heart of it, life with animals is not about grandeur or glory. It's about the small moments: a soft nose in your hand, a wagging tail, a shared look that needs no words.

And that, I think, is the happiest ending anyone could wish for.

Printed in Dunstable, United Kingdom